# Union-Castle Line In Colour

By

Barry J. Eagles

**For my children, James and Charlotte**

First Published 2001    ISBN 0 946184 92 5

*Front cover:* The Union-Castle liner *Durham Castle,* taken from a postcard.

Union-Castle
Line.

Published By

## Waterfront

A Division of Kingfisher Productions

The Dalesmade Centre, Watershed Mill, Settle,

North Yorkshire BD24 9LR

Printed by The Amadeus Press, Cleckheaton, West Yorkshire

TYPES OF THE SHIPS OF THE
UNION-CASTLE LINE
ROYAL MAIL AND INTERMEDIATE SERVICES
To SOUTH & EAST AFRICA

# Introduction

I have always been fascinated by postcards of ships and trains and I am an avid collector of them. In the 1960s I saw many ocean liners at Southampton Docks and I was given many postcards by people including my father, James Eagles, who worked as an electrician there for many years. He obtained a Southern Railway clock for me, which used to be in the pumping station at the King George the Fifth Graving Dock, for the princely sum of ten shillings (50 pence)! It ticks away in my railway room, keeping perfect time, as it has since it was made 70 years ago. Its ticking inspires this forward and takes one back to the heyday of the great Cunarders and other shipping companies and in particular to my favourite shipping company, the Union-Castle Line. This company was formed in 1900 by the amalgamation of the Union and Castle Lines. Its beautiful "lavender hulled lovelies", with red and black funnels, were a familiar sight in Southampton Docks as they arrived and departed to and from South Africa. My clock may have had its time checked at four o'clock on a Thursday, when a Union-Castle liner departed on its long way to Capetown. In 1965 the service was speeded up with ships leaving at one o'clock on a Friday. Like most liner travel, in 1977 the service came to an end and the mailboats were withdrawn. Southampton was a sadder place without them. Whilst working for an American company, I had many "Poets" (pushed off early tomorrows Saturday) so I could get to Hythe Pier to photograph or just watch a mailboat sail by. On numerous occasions I would go out on the Red Funnel tug *Thorness*, or the tug tender *Calshot* (the successor to the preserved *Calshot*), at the invitation of my good friends Captain George Howard and Captain Steve Pascoe, both sadly now passed over the bar. They were very experienced tug skippers and I used to marvel as they let go as the mighty ships bore down on them.

The Union-Castle Company issued many postcards in its years of existence, the great majority being in a sepia or black and white form. What has surprised me is the number of coloured postcards that were issued. It is these that form the basis of this book. My favourite postcards are the ones of Franchis Godolphin Osborne Stuart. He started issuing postcards of local scenes, including shipping in 1901. Two years later he sold postcards which he had

A large crowd watches as the *Athlone Castle* (page 46) arrives in Capetown harbour. What a wonderful scene. Table Mountain dominates the whole view.

colour lithographed in Germany. These of course came to a rapid end in 1914 and his beautifully coloured postcards disappeared. In the market place they now demand more than the cost of this book! Several F.G.O. Stuart postcards are included here. The publishers Salmon of Sevenoaks produced postcards of liners, including some Union-Castle ones. Some of the later mailboats were captured on colour film and printed as postcards by the Isle of Wight firm of J. Arthur Dixon. All of these cards are highly collectable nowadays.

A lot of postcards had interesting messages written by long-dead hands. These make interesting reading now and show how the times have changed – and not necessarily for the better! One message tells a girlfriend that her young man would not be able to see her that evening. This was posted in the morning to arrive second delivery at mid-day. I am lucky if I get my first and only delivery by mid-day!

In recent years my postcard collecting has been rather spasmodic with the high cost of purcashing them, but I have managed to find

Union Castle Liner, R.M.S. "Walmer Castle"

The **TECHNICAL DETAILS** are given as the ship was built. These would have altered after refits. In some instances the gross registered tonnage given will differ from that on the postcard.

Ships classified as mail boats sailed from Southampton to Capetown. Some went on to Port Elizabeth, East London and Durban. Some ships called at Las Palmas and Madiera. Ships on the intermediate service sailed from London through the Mediterranean, Suez Canel to Mombasa and Durban. Round Africa service was from London via Suez , Eastern coast of South Africa and back via Capetown to London.

Union-Castle Line.

*Left:* A postcard of the *Walmer Castle* (page 23) posted in Kingsbridge on 9th March 1906. This was published by Valentine's.

*Below:* A very colourful postcard view of the motorship *Dunbar Castle* (page 42).

some Union-Castle postcards in that beautiful country of South Africa, on some of my many visits there. The last postcards I bought, at a reasonable price, were near a town called Waikanae in North Island, New Zealand although passenger mailboats never called there. On the long flight from Auckland to Heathrow, via Los Angeles, the passenger who was sitting next to me remarked on the shipping book that I was reading and struck up a conversation with me. He told me that he was a retired Australian customs officer and that he did not know what to do with the many postcards he had collected from ships in Sydney Harbour. He now sends shipping postcards to me in exchange for English Commemorative stamps.

I must thank my friends; John Lindsay and Peter Harris, for letting me browse through their collections. Some of their cards are illustrated in this album. I also thank my publisher Roger Hardingham for his enthusiasm and my wife Carol who shares my love of South Africa, shipping and the sea.
**Barry J. Eagles, Chandlers Ford, Hampshire**

The UNION-CASTLE Intermediate Motorship "DUNBAR CASTLE" (1000? tons)

# DUNNOTTAR CASTLE

*Dunnottar Castle* was the first two-funnelled Castle ship. She was built by the Fairfield Ship Building and Engineering Company of Glasgow and was launched on the 22nd May 1890. In August of that year she undertook a cruise for her owner Donald Currie and it was not until the 28th October 1890 that she arrived at Capetown for the first time. She held the record for the fastest ship on the Cape run for nearly a year. *Dunnottar Castle* carried troops and Mr Winston Churchill to Capetown in October 1899 at the beginning of the Boer War. In 1900 she became the first vessel to fly the Union- Castle house flag. With the amalgamation of the Union- and Castle Line, she became redundant and from 1904 to 1907 was laid up at Netley. In June 1907 she was chartered to the Panama Railroad Company for service between New York and Panama. Two years later she was cruising to Norway and the Mediterranean, for a Sir Henry Lunn. A change of name occurred in April 1913 when she was sold to the Royal Mail Steam Packet Company and renamed *Caribbean*. She was called up for war service in 1914 and she became a troopship and then an armed merchant cruiser. In June 1915 she was purchased by the Admiralty for use as an accommodation ship. Her end came on the 27th September 1915 when she sank off of Cape Wrath whilst on her way to Scapa Flow.

**TECHNICAL DETAILS.** Powered by a triple expansion steam engine, developing 6,700 indicated horse power, driving a single screw, giving a maximum speed of 16 knots. Her length was 420 feet with a gross registered tonnage of 5,465. She carried 370 passengers in three classes. *Dunnottar Castle* was named after a castle one mile south of Stonehaven in Grampian.

Union-Castle Line.

Union Castle Liner, R.M.S. "Scot"

# SCOT

*Scot* was the first Union liner to have twin screws. She was built by William Denny of Dumbarton and launched on the 30th December 1890. She arrived at Capetown for the first time on the 10th August 1891 and bettered *Dunnottar Castle's* (page 4) record for the fastest time on the Southbound run. *Scot* held the record for the fastest passage for the next 45 years. In 1896 she was sent to Harland and Wolff of Belfast for refitting and was lengthened by 54 feet. Her last arrival at Southampton was on the 12th September 1903. She was laid up at Netley for two years before being sold to the Hamburg America Line in October 1905 for conversion to a cruise liner, by Harland and Wolff of Belfast and renamed the *Oceana*. Six years later she was sold to the Bermuda Atlantic Steamship Company of Toronto. This service proved to be a failure and *Oceana* was laid up till 1914. She was then chartered to the Bermuda American Company Limited. This company went bankrupt and *Oceana* was sold yet again. On the 22nd September 1915 the Compania Trasatlantica of Barcelona bought her and renamed her *Alfonso XIII*. This name was retained until November 1923 when she received her final name *Vasco Nunez de Balbao*. Her service was from Cadiz to Havana. She was sold after a two year lay up in Cadiz to shipbreakers in La Spezia and arrived there for breaking-up on the 6th July 1927.

**TECHNICAL DETAILS.** Powered by triple expansion steam engines, developing 11,000 indicated horse power driving twin screws, giving a maximum speed of 18 knots. Her length when built, was 477 feet with a gross registered tonnage of 6,844. She carried 425 passengers in three classes.   Postcard published by Valentines.

# GAUL

*Gaul* was the first of the 'G' class, built for the Union Line. She was built by Harland and Wolff of Belfast and was launched on the 16th of February 1893. *Gaul* made her maiden arrival at Capetown on the 10th June 1893. She was sold to the Royal Mail Steam Packet Company in 1906 for that company's service from Southampton to Cuba and Mexico and renamed *Sabor*. In June 1909 *Sabor* was transferred to the Shire Line and renamed *Carmarthenshire* and used on that line's Far Eastern routes. Four years later she was placed on the service from Canada to the West Indies and her name changed yet again to *Chaleur*. She was sold in July 1927 and a month later she arrived at Rotterdam for breaking-up.

**TECHNICAL DETAILS.** Powered by triple expansion steam engines, developing 2,200 indicated horse power, driving twin screws giving a maximum speed of 11½ knots. Her length was 400 feet 6 inches, with a gross registered tonnage of 4,745. She carried 163 passengers in three classes. Postcard published by F.G.O. Stuart.

Union-Castle
Line.

Union-Castle
Line.

UNION CASTLE LINE S. S. "GREEK"

# GREEK

*Greek* was the third of the 'G' class built for the Union Line. She was built by Harland and Wolff of Belfast and launched on the 18th May 1893. *Greek* arrived at Capetown for the first time on the 17th October 1893. She was sold along with her sister *Gaul* (page 6) in March 1906 to the Royal Mail Steam Packet Company for that company's service from Southampton to Cuba and Mexico and renamed *Segura*. Her career after leaving the Union Line was identical to that of the *Gaul*. She was transferred to the Shire Line in June 1909 and renamed *Pembrokeshire*. In 1913 she was transferred to the Royal Mail Steam Packet's Canada to the West Indies service and renamed *Chignecto*. This service came to an end in 1927. *Chignecto* was sold with her sister, the former *Gaul* to Dutch ship breakers and was towed to Rotterdam for breaking-up.

**TECHNICAL DETAILS.** Identical to the *Gaul* (page 6), except her gross registered tonnage was 4,757.   Postcard published by F.G.O. Stuart.

THE UNION-CASTLE LINE INTERMEDIATE STEAMER "GUELPH" (4917 TONS)

# GUELPH

*Guelph* was the fourth member of the 'G' class built for the Union Line. She was built by Harland and Wolff of Belfast and was launched on the 26th June 1894. *Guelph* made her maiden arrival at Capetown on the 29th October 1894. She had three masts instead of the two her earlier sisters had. In 1913 she was transferred to the Royal Mail Steam Packet and renamed *Caraquet*. As this she was employed on that company's Canada to the West Indies service. On the 25th June 1923 she was wrecked on a reef near Hamilton, Bermuda, fortunately without loss of life. Her name *Guelph* was the family name of Queen Victoria.

**TECHNICAL DETAILS.** Identical to the *Gaul* (page 6) except her gross registered tonnage was 4,917 and she carried 194 passengers in three classes.   Postcard published by the Union-Castle Line.

Union-Castle
Line.

Union-Castle
Line.

Union-Castle
Line.

S.S. NORMAN off SWANAGE.

# NORMAN (2)

*Norman* (2), the second ship of that name built for the Union Line, gave that line and its successor Union-Castle, 32 years of faithful service. She was built by Harland and Wolff of Belfast and launched on the 18th July 1894. Her first arrival at Capetown was on the 26th November 1894. Apart from a grounding in July 1895, she had an uneventful life until she was laid up at Netley in 1911. *Norman* (2) was reactivated in August 1914 and resumed her service on the Cape run. In 1917 she was requisitioned as a troopship and served in the Mediterranean. *Norman* (2) was transferred to the Round Africa service in 1923. She served on this route for a few more years, until March 1926, when she arrived at the Morecambe yard of T. W. Ward for breaking-up.

**TECHNICAL DETAILS.** Powered by triple expansion steam engines developing 9,000 indicated horse power, driving twin screws, giving a maximum speed of 17 knots. Her length was 490 feet 8 inches with a gross registered tonnage of 7,537. She carried 442 passengers in three classes.

Postcard is from a painting by Neville Cumming published by Raphael Tuck and Sons in the Oilette Series.

UNION CASTLE LINE S. S. "ARUNDEL CASTLE"

# ARUNDEL CASTLE (2)

*Arundel Castle* (2) was the second ship of that name built for the Castle Line. She was built by the Fairfield Ship Building and Engineering Company of Glasgow and was launched on the 2nd October 1894. Her maiden arrival at Capetown was on the 9th May 1895. She was an early casualty of the merger of the Union and Castle Lines, being sold in May 1905 to the East Asiatic Company of Copenhagen. She was renamed *Birma* and remained under the Danish flag for a period of four years. In 1909 she was transferred to the Russian flag. In 1914 she was renamed *Mitau*, and she was laid up in St Petersburg for the duration of the First World War. *Mitau* was sold in February 1921 to the Polish Navigation Company and renamed *Jozef Piludski*. This name change was short lived and in 1923 she was sold to Hellmers of Kiel and renamed *Franck Hellmers*. A year later she was renamed *Wilbo*. This was to be the final name change as on the 10th December 1924 she arrived at Genoa for breaking-up.

**TECHNICAL DETAILS.** Powered by a triple expansion steam engine developing 3,300 indicated horse power, driving a single screw, giving a maximum speed of 13 knots. Her length was 415 feet, with a gross registered tonnage of 4,588. She carried 370 passengers in three classes.
*Arundel Castle* was named after the castle in Sussex, the home of the Dukes of Norfolk. Postcard published by F.G.O. Stuart.

S.S. DUNVEGAN CASTLE leaving TABLE BAY.

# DUNVEGAN CASTLE

*Dunvegan Castle* was already obsolete when built. She was built by the Fairfield Ship Building and Engineering Company Limited of Glasgow and was launched on the 14th April 1896. Her maiden arrival at Capetown was on the 22nd September 1896. Six years later, in October 1902, she collided with the Victoria Basin at Capetown causing £10,000 of damage. *Dunvegan Castle* was placed in the reserve fleet in May 1904. In September 1913 after service on the London to Durban route she was placed on the sales list, but with the advent of the First World War she was requisitioned by the Admiralty. She was at first utilised as a troopship until conversion in 1915 into a hospital ship. A year later, in 1916, she resumed her service on the Cape mail route. In 1923 she was sold for breaking-up in Kiel.

**TECHNICAL DETAILS.** Powered by a triple expansion steam engine, developing 7,000 indicated horse power, driving a single screw, giving a maximum speed of 16 knots. Her length was 450 feet 6 inches with a gross registered tonnage of 5,958. She carried 513 passengers in three classes.
*Dunvegan Castle* was named after a castle on the Isle of Skye, the home of the Chieftains of the Clan Macleod.
Postcard is from a painting by Neville Cumming published by Raphael Tuck and Sons in the Oilette Series.

THE UNION-CASTLE LINE INTERMEDIATE STEAMER "GASCON" (6288 TONS)

# GASCON (2)

*Gascon* (2) was the first of a larger 'G' 'class built for the Union Lines intermediate service. She was built by Harland and Wolff of Belfast and launched on the 25th August 1896. Her first call at Capetown was on the 11th April 1897. In 1905 *Gascon* (2) made the first Union Castle call at Lobito in Angola. On the 20th September 1914 she picked up survivors from *H.M.S. Pegasus* which had been sunk by the German cruiser *Konigsberg*. *Gascon* (2) was used as a hospital ship for the remainder of the First World War and she was not returned to her owners until the 29th July 1920. In 1926 she was laid up in Southampton Water for a period of nine months before purchase by T. W. Ward and arrived at Inverkeithing for breaking-up in September 1928.

**TECHNICAL DETAILS.** Powered by triple expansion steam engines, developing 2,750 indicated horse power, driving twin screws, giving a maximum speed of 11½ knots. Her length was 430 feet with a gross registered tonnage of 6,278. She carried 242 passengers in three classes.   Postcard published by the Union-Castle Line.

UNION-CASTLE LINE INTERMEDIATE STEAMER "GAIKA."   6,287 TONS.

# GAIKA

*Gaika* was the second of the new 'G 'class built for the Union Line. She was built by Harland and Wolff of Belfast and launched on the 22nd September 1896. She was identical to the *Gascon* (2) (page 12). *Gaika* arrived at Capetown for the first time on the 23rd May 1897. In November 1902 she ran aground at Las Palmas and had to return to England for repairs. She carried troops from Capetown to German South West Africa in 1914. In 1917 she was requisitioned by the Shipping Controller and used on the Australian route for two years. *Gaika* was laid up in Southampton Water and then London's East India Dock for three years before being sold for breaking-up in Savona, where she arrived in March 1929.

**TECHNICAL DETAILS.** Identical to *Gascon* (2) except she carried 240 passengers in three classes.

F. G. O. Stuart. 1356

Union Castle Line S. S. Avondale Castle

# AVONDALE CASTLE

*Avondale Castle* was built for the Castle Line's intermediate service. She was built by the Fairfield Ship Building and Engineering Company of Glasgow and launched on the 5th November 1896. Her maiden arrival at Capetown was on the 22nd February 1897. *Avondale Castle* was sold to the Cie de Nav Sud Atlantique of Bordeaux in August 1912 and renamed *Carronna*. She was used on the service from Bordeaux to South America for ten years before being broken up in Bordeaux in 1923.

**TECHNICAL DETAILS**. Powered by a triple expansion steam engine, developing 3,500 indicated horse power, driving a single screw, giving a maximum speed of 14 knots. Her length was 425 feet 2 inches with a gross registered tonnage of 5,513. She carried 326 passengers in three classes.
*Avondale Castle* was named after a castle in the town of Strathaven in Strathclyde. Postcard published F.G.O. Stuart.

Union Castle Line Royal Mail Steamer "Briton"

F. G. O. Stuart. 136

# BRITON (3)

*Briton* (3) was the third ship of that name built for the Union Line and was the first mailship over 10,000 gross registered tonnage. She was built by Harland and Wolff of Belfast and was launched on the 5th June 1897. Her first arrival at Capetown was on the 21st December 1897. In October 1899 she carried 1,500 troops to Capetown to fight in the Boer War and then returned to her civilian duties on the mail route. *Briton* (3) was requisitioned as a troopship at the beginning of the First World War, but after only six weeks she was returned to the mail run. On the 16th December 1915 she was again requisitioned as a troopship and this time was not demobilised until 1920. In January 1925 she was laid up at Netley and after making one last round trip to the Cape, she arrived at La Spezia in May 1926 for breaking-up.

**TECHNICAL DETAILS.** Powered by triple expansion steam engines, developing 10,500 indicated horse power, driving twin screws, giving a maximum speed of 17½ knots. Her length was 530 feet 3 inches with a gross registered tonnage of 10,248. She carried 584 passengers in three classes.   Postcard published by F.G.O. Stuart.

71    Union Castle Line R. M. S. "Carisbrook Castle"

# CARISBROOK CASTLE

*Carisbrook Castle* was the last of the Castle Line single screw mail ships. She was built by the Fairfield Ship Building and Engineering Company Limited of Glasgow and was launched on the 28th October 1897. Her first arrival at Capetown was on the 28th June 1898. In 1913 she was placed on the route from London to Durban via the Suez Canal. She was requisitioned as a hospital ship by the Admiralty at the beginning of the First World War and served in the Mediterranean and on the cross channel ambulance service. *Carisbrook Castle* was not returned to her owners until August 1919. In 1922 she was laid up on the River Blackwater and in October of that year she was sold for breaking-up in Germany.

**TECHNICAL DETAILS.** Powered by a triple expansion steam engine, developing 9,000 indicated horse power, driving a single screw, giving a maximum speed of 18 knots. Her length was 485 feet with a gross registered tonnage of 7,626. She carried 620 passengers in three classes.
*Carisbrook Castle* was named after a castle on the Isle of Wight near Newport (actually spelt Carisbroke Castle).
Postcard published by F.G.O. Stuart.

Union-Castle Line.

UNION-CASTLE LINE INTERMEDIATE STEAMER "BRAEMAR CASTLE," 6266 TONS.

# BRAEMAR CASTLE

*Braemar Castle* was the last Castle Line single screw intermediate ship. She was built by Barclay Curlé and Company of Whiteinch and was launched on the 23rd February 1898. Her maiden arrival at Capetown was on the 4th September 1898. In 1909 she was chartered as a troopship and during the First World War became a hospital ship. On the 23rd November 1916 she hit a mine in the Mykonos Channel, which resulted in the loss of four lives. She was refloated and towed to Malta for repairs, but was eventually repaired at La Spezia. *Braemar Castle* became a base hospital at Murmansk in 1918. In 1920 she made a voyage on the intermediate run to the Cape. Two years later she took part in a peace keeping force in the war between Greece and Turkey. On the 12th October 1924 *Braemar Castle* arrived at Genoa for breaking-up.

**TECHNICAL DETAILS.** Powered by a quadruple expansion steam engine, developing 4,400 indicated horse power, driving a single screw, giving a maximum speed of 15 knots. Her length was 450 feet with a gross registered tonnage of 6,266. She carried 360 passengers in three classes.
*Braemar Castle* was named after a castle overlooking the River Dee in Grampian.

UNION-CASTLE LINE INTERMEDIATE STEAMER ▬▬▬▬ 6,769 TONS.

"GLENGORM CASTLE."

# GLENGORM CASTLE

*Glengorm Castle* was a member of the 'G' class and was built as the *German*. She was built by Harland and Wolff of Belfast and launched on the 4th August 1898. Her maiden arrival at Capetown was on the 29th January 1899. A few days after completion, on the 16th November 1898, she sank the Wilson Lines *Corso* in the River Elbe. At the outbreak of the First World War she was requisitioned and converted into a hospital ship and for obvious reasons her name was changed from *German* to the *Glengorm Castle*. She served as a hospital ship for seven years and then another four years as a troop ship. It was not until 1925 that she was demobilised and resumed her service on the intermediate route. In March 1930 *Glengorm Castle* was sold to a Dutch ship breaker and on the 11th April 1930 left London for breaking-up near Rotterdam. She was the last survivor of the first 'G' class.

**TECHNICAL DETAILS.** Powered by triple expansion steam engines, developing 2,900 indicated horse power, driving twin screws, giving a maximum speed of 12 knots. Her length was 440 feet 3 inches with a gross registered tonnage of 6,763. She carried 279 passengers in three classes. *Glengorm Castle* was named after a castle on the Isle of Mull.

Union Castle Line Royal Mail Steamer "Kinfauns Castle"

F.G.O. Stuart. 188

# KINFAUNS CASTLE (2)

*Kinfauns Castle* (2), the second ship of that name built for the Castle Line, was that line's first twin screw ship. She was built by the Fairfield Ship Building and Engineering Company of Glasgow and was launched on the 12th May 1899. Her maiden arrival at Capetown was on the 18th October 1899. *Kinfauns Castle* (2) was requisitioned by the Admiralty at the beginning of the First World War and from the 5th August 1914 to the 16th September 1915 she served as an armed merchant cruiser. She was then converted into a troopship and was returned to the Union-Castle Line in February 1919. On the 8th September 1922 she helped to rescue passengers and crew from the German Liner *Hammonia*. *Kinfauns Castle* was laid up at the end of 1922 at Netley. She was not reactivated until October 1925, when she made a final voyage to Capetown. In September 1927 she was sold for breaking-up near Rotterdam.

**TECHNICAL DETAILS.** Powered by quadruple expansion steam engines, developing 9,800 indicated horse power, driving twin screws, giving a maximum speed of 18 knots. Her length was 515 feet 3 inches with a gross registered tonnage of 9,664. She carried 635 passengers in three classes.
*Kinfauns Castle* (2) was named after a folly built in 1822 on the Tayside.   Postcard published by F.G.O. Stuart.

UNION-CASTLE LINE ROYAL MAIL STEAMER "KILDONAN CASTLE." 9,692 TONS.

# KILDONAN CASTLE

*Kildonan Castle* the sister ship of the *Kinfauns Castle* (2) (page 19) was the last ship built for the Castle Line. She was built by the Fairfield Ship Building and Engineering Company and was launched on the 22nd August 1899. She was immediately requisitioned as a troop transport for the Boer War. *Kildonan Castle* carried 20,429 troops from the 5th October 1899 to the 23rd May 1901. Her maiden arrival at Capetown was on the 22nd November 1899. In 1915 she was requisitioned by the Admiralty for service in the First World War and from the 6th October 1915 to the 10th March 1916, she served as a hospital ship. *Kildonan Castle* spent the rest of the war as an armed merchant cruiser and it was not until the 31st December 1921 that she was returned to the Union-Castle Line. She remained on the mail route for another five years and she then became a reserve ship. On the 18th May 1930 she arrived at Stavanger for breaking-up.

**TECHNICAL DETAILS.** Identical to *Kinfauns Castle* (2) (page 19) except gross registered tonnage was 9,652. *Kildonan Castle* was named after a castle on the Isle of Arran.

UNION-CASTLE LINE INTERMEDIATE STEAMER "GALEKA." 6,772 TONS.

# GALEKA

*Galeka* was a member of the Union Line 'G' class and she was the last ship to fly the Union Line flag. She was built by Harland and Wolff of Belfast and was launched on the 21st October 1899. Her first arrival at Capetown was on the 28th January 1900. On the 7th August 1914 *Galeka* was requisitioned as a troopship and during June 1915 she was converted into a hospital ship. On the 28th October 1916 *Galeka* struck a mine near Le Havre and became a total loss.

**TECHNICAL DETAILS.** Identical to the *Glengorm Castle* (page 18) except gross registered tonnage was 6,767 and she carried 309 passengers in three classes.

S.S. SAXON passing the NEEDLES.

# SAXON (4)

*Saxon* (4) was the last mailship built for the Union Line. She was built by Harland and Wolff of Belfast and launched on the 21st December 1899. Her maiden arrival at Capetown was on the 3rd July 1900. She was requisitioned as a troopship in 1916 serving in the Mediterranean and the North Atlantic carrying troops from the United States. In 1919 *Saxon* (4) was released from war service and resumed her duties on the mail service. In August 1921, after departure from Madeira, a fire broke out in her coal bunkers and her voyage had to be terminated at Freetown, Sierra Leone. She remained on the mail service until April 1931, and was then laid up at Netley. *Saxon* (4) was sold for breaking-up and on the 9th April 1935 she arrived at Hughes Bolckow ship breaking yard at Blyth.

**TECHNICAL DETAILS.** Powered by quadruple expansion steam engines, developing 11,800 indicated horse power, driving twin screws, giving a maximum speed of 17½ knots. Her length was 570 feet 5 inches with a gross registered tonnage of 12,385. She carried 799 passengers in three classes. Postcard is from a painting by Neville Cumming published by Raphael Tuck and Sons in the Oilette Series.

UNION-CASTLE LINE ROYAL MAIL STEAMER "WALMER CASTLE."    12,546 TONS.

# WALMER CASTLE

*Walmer Castle* was originally laid down as the *Celt* (3) for the Union Line. She was built by Harland and Wolff of Belfast and was launched on the 6th July 1901. Her maiden arrival at Capetown was on the 1st April 1902. She was requisitioned as a troop ship in April 1917 and was used to transport troops from the United States across the Atlantic. *Walmer Castle* was returned to her owners in 1919. In January 1931 she was laid up at Netley and sold for breaking-up. She arrived on the 8th February 1932 at the Hughes Bolckow ship breaking yard at Blyth.

**TECHNICAL DETAILS.** Powered by quadruple expansion steam engines, developing 12,000 indicated horse power, driving twin screws, giving a maximum speed of 16½ knots. Her length was 570 feet 5 inches with a gross registered tonnage of 12,546. She carried 754 passengers in three classes.
*Walmer Castle* was named after a castle in Kent the official residence of the Lord Warden of the cinque ports.
Postcard publisher unknown.  Postcard published by Valentines.

# ARMADALE CASTLE

*Armadale Castle* was built as a replacement for the *Scot* (page 5). She was built by the Fairfield Ship Building and Engineering Company of Glasgow and was launched on the 11th August 1903. Her maiden arrival at Capetown was on the 22nd December 1903. She was requisitioned by the Admiralty on the 2nd August 1914 and served as an armed merchant cruiser for the duration of the First World War. *Armadale Castle* was returned to her owners on the 11th September 1919 and was refitted on the Clyde before resuming her service on the Cape run. She served the Union-Castle Line for the next 17 years and it was not until the 12th June 1936 that she arrived at Hughes Bolckow yard at Blyth for breaking-up.

**TECHNICAL DETAILS.** Powered by quadruple expansion steam engines, developing 12,500 indicated horse power, driving twin screws, giving a maximum speed of 16½ knots. Her length was 570 feet 1 inch with a gross registered tonnage of 12,973. She carried 820 passengers in three classes.
*Armadale Castle* was named after a castle on the Isle of Skye. Postcard published by J.W.B. of London in their Commercial Series.

Union-Castle
Line.

S.S. KENILWORTH CASTLE
in the CHANNEL.

# KENILWORTH CASTLE (2)

*Kenilworth Castle* (2) was the second ship of that name built for the Cape route. She was built by Harland and Wolff of Belfast she was launched on the 5th December 1903. Her first arrival at Capetown was on the 14th June 1904. On the 11th August 1914 she was requisitioned by the Admiralty and converted into a troopship. On the 4th June 1918 she collided with and cut in two, the destroyer *H.M.S. Rival* off Plymouth with the loss of 15 lives. *Kenilworth Castle* (2) was demobilised in 1919 and served on the mail service for the next 17 years until she was replaced by the *Stirling Castle* (2) (page 45). She was sold to Hughes Bolckow and arrived at their Blyth yard for breaking-up on the 8th January 1937.

**TECHNICAL DETAILS.** Powered by quadruple expansion steam engines, developing 12,000 indicated horse power, driving twin screws, giving a maximum speed of 16½ knots. Her length was 570 feet 2 inches with a gross registered tonnage of 12,974. She carried 794 passengers in three classes.
*Kenilworth Castle* (2) was named after a castle in Warwickshire. Postcard is from a painting by Neville Cumming published by Raphael Tuck and Sons in the Oilette Series.

UNION-CASTLE LINE INTERMEDIATE STEAMER "DURHAM CASTLE."    8,217 TONS.

# DURHAM CASTLE

*Durham Castle* was the first of the 'D' class of West Coast intermediate ships. She was built by the Fairfield Ship Building and Engineering Company of Glasgow and was launched on the 17th December 1903. Her first arrival at Capetown was on the 10th April 1904. *Durham Castle* remained on the intermediate service during the First World War. During November 1931 she was placed on the Union-Castle Round-Africa service. She was sold to Metal Industries Limited of Rosyth for breaking-up in June 1939, but instead was requisitioned by the Admiralty. *Durham Castle* was to have been used as a blockship at Scapa Flow, but on the 26th January 1940 she struck a mine and sunk off Cromarty.

**TECHNICAL DETAILS.** Powered by quadruple expansion steam engines, developing 5,200 indicated horse power, driving twin screws, giving a maximum speed of 13 knots. Her length was 475 feet 4 inches with a gross registered tonnage of 8,217. She carried 800 passengers in three classes.
*Durham Castle* was named after a castle now part of Durham University.  Postcard·published by F.G.O. Stuart.

UNION-CASTLE LINE INTERMEDIATE STEAMER "DOVER CASTLE." (8,200 TONS.)

# DOVER CASTLE (2)

*Dover Castle* (2) only the second ship of that name had a short life of 13 years. She was built by Barclay Curlé and Company Limited of Whiteinch, and she was launched on the 4th February 1904. Her maiden arrival at Capetown was on the 22nd May 1904. On the 2nd September 1914 she was requisitioned by the Admiralty and converted into a hospital ship. *Dover Castle* (2) was torpedoed and sunk by the German submarine UC 67 off the coast of Algiers on the 26th May 1917.

**TECHNICAL DETAILS.** Identical to *Durham Castle* (page 26) except her length was 476 feet 4 inches, with a gross registered tonnage of 8,271. *Dover Castle* (2) was named after the castle overlooking Dover harbour in Kent.

UNION-CASTLE LINE ROYAL MAIL STEAMER "DUNLUCE CASTLE."   8,500 TONS.

# DUNLUCE CASTLE.

*Dunluce Castle* was the third and last of the 'D' class built for the intermediate service. She was built by Harland and Wolff of Belfast and was launched on the 31st April 1904. Her maiden arrival at Capetown was on the 6th November 1904. She was requisitioned on the 6th July 1915 and converted into a hospital ship. She served in the Mediterranean and it was not until 1920 that she was demobilised and returned to her owner's intermediate service. In June 1939 she was bought for breaking up by Smith and Houston Limited of Port Glasgow. With the advent of the Second World War, she was requisitioned by the Admiralty for a second time. *Dunluce Castle* was used as an accommodation ship at Immingham and then a depot ship at Scapa Flow. In July 1945 she was bought by T. W. Ward for breaking-up at Inverkeithing.

**TECHNICAL DETAILS.** Identical to *Durham Castle* (page 26) except gross registered tonnage was 8,114.
*Dunluce Castle* was named after a castle in Co. Antrim, Northern Ireland.

THE UNION-CASTLE LINE INTERMEDIATE STEAMER "GRANTULLY CASTLE" (7612 TON

# GRANTULLY CASTLE

*Grantully Castle* was the first of the new 'G' class built for the intermediate service. She was built by Barclay Curlé and Company of Whiteinch and launched on the 11th October 1909. Her first arrival at Capetown was on the 14th February 1910. During the First World War she was requisitioned by the Admiralty and converted into a hospital ship. She served in that capacity from the 22nd June 1915 to the 11th March 1919. *Grantully Castle* was demobilised and returned to Union-Castle in September 1919. Between periods of lay-up she gave her owners another 20 years of service. She was sold to P. W. Maclellan Limited and on the 20th July 1939 she arrived at Bo'ness for breaking up.

**TECHNICAL DETAILS.** Powered by quadruple expansion steam engines, developing 3,250 indicated horse power, driving twin screws, giving a maximum speed of 12 knots. Her length was 450 feet 7 inches with a gross registered tonnage of 7,606. She carried 379 passengers in three classes. *Grantully Castle* was named after a castle in Perthshire.

UNION-CASTLE LINE ROYAL MAIL STEAMER "BALMORAL CASTLE." 13,361 TONS.

# BALMORAL CASTLE (2)

*Balmoral Castle* (2) the second ship of that name built for the mail run, was a larger version of the Walmer *Castle* (page 23). She was built by the Fairfield Ship Building and Engineering Company of Glasgow and was launched on the 13th November 1909. Her maiden arrival at Capetown was on the 19th April 1910. In October of that year she was commissioned as a royal yacht and she carried the Duke and Duchess of Connaught to South Africa. At the beginning of the First World War *Balmoral* Castle (2) was briefly commissioned as a troopship. She soon returned to the Cape mail run and it was not until 1917 that she was again requisitioned as a troopship for transporting United States troops across the Atlantic. During 1919 she was returned to the Union-Castle Line and remained on this service for another 20 years. She was then withdrawn from service and sold to Cashmores Limited. On the 19th June 1939 *Balmoral Castle* (2) arrived at Cashmores Newport yard for breaking-up.

**TECHNICAL DETAILS.** Powered by quadruple expansion steam engines, developing 12,500 indicated horse power, driving twin screws, giving a maximum speed of 16½ knots. Her length was 570 feet with a gross registered tonnage of 13,361. She carried 805 passengers in three classes. *Balmoral Castle* (2) was named after a castle on the banks of the River Dee in Grampian, bought by Queen Victoria.

UNION-CASTLE LINE INTERMEDIATE STEAMER "GARTH CASTLE." 7,610 TONS.

# GARTH CASTLE (2)

*Garth Castle* (2) was the second ship of that name built for the intermediate service. She was built by Barclay Curlé and Company of Whiteinch and was launched on the 13th January 1910. Her maiden arrival at Capetown was on the 25th April 1910. She was requisitioned by the Admiralty on the 4th November 1914 and converted to a hospital ship, based at Scapa Flow. *Garth Castle* (2) was released to the Union-Castle Line on the 24th October 1919, and resumed her duties on the intermediate route. On the 25th March 1926 she ran aground off the Island of Ascension and her passengers had to be transferred to the *Kenilworth Castle* (page 25), whilst she proceeded to Capetown for repairs. *Garth Castle* (2) was sold to Hughes Bolckow and on the 14th June 1939 arrived at their Blyth yard for breaking-up.

**TECHNICAL DETAILS.** Identical to *Grantully Castle* (page 29) except her length was 452 feet 6 inches with a gross registered tonnage of 7,610.
*Garth Castle* (2) was named after Sir Donald Currie's (born 1825, died 1909 managing director of the Union-Castle Line) estate near Fortingall on Tayside.

F. G. O. Stuart. 1735      Union-Castle Line R. M. S. Edinburgh Castle

# EDINBURGH CASTLE (2)

*Edinburgh Castle* (2) was the second ship of that name built for the Cape run and was a sister ship of *Balmoral Castle* (2) (page 30). She was built by Harland and Wolff of Belfast and she was launched on the 27th January 1910. Her maiden arrival at Capetown was on the 7th June 1910. On the 4th September 1914 she was requisitioned by the Admiralty and commissioned as an armed merchant cruiser. She served on convoy duty in the Atlantic and it was not until the 12th July 1919 that she was demobilised and was refitted at Belfast after which she resumed her duties on the Cape run. *Edinburgh Castle* (2) made her last departure from Capetown on the 19th January 1939 and was requisitioned again by the Admiralty and used as an accommodation ship at Freetown, Sierra Leone. She remained there for the duration of the Second World War and on the 24th November 1945 she was towed out to sea and sunk by gunfire from vessels of the Royal Navy.

**TECHNICAL DETAILS.** Identical to *Balmoral Castle* (2) except gross registered tonnage was 13,330 and she carried 790 passengers in three classes. *Edinburgh Castle* (2) was named after the castle overlooking the City of Edinburgh in Lothian. Postcard published by F.G.O. Stuart.

Union-Castle
Line.

Union-Castle
Line.

THE UNION CASTLE LINE INTERMEDIATE STEAMER
GALWAY CASTLE (7988 TONS)

# GALWAY CASTLE

*Galway Castle* was the final member of the second 'G' class built for the west coast intermediate route. She was built by Harland and Wolff of Belfast and launched on the 12th April 1911. Her first arrival at Capetown was on the 19th November 1911. She was used briefly as a troopship in September 1914 transporting troops from Capetown to German South West Africa, and then returned to the Cape run. On the 12th October 1917 she ran aground at East London and was refloated a few days later. *Galway Castle* was torpedoed by the German submarine, U82, 160 miles south of the Fastnet Rock, on the 12th September 1918. She took three days to sink but unfortunately 150 lives were lost. *Galway Castle* had a brief life of only seven years.

**TECHNICAL DETAILS.** Powered by quadruple expansion steam engines, developing 3,750 indicated horse power, driving twin screws, giving a maximum speed of 12 knots. Her length was 452 feet 3 inches with a gross registered tonnage of 7,988. She carried 312 passengers in three classes.
*Galway Castle* was named after a castle in Co Galway, Eire, the ancestral home of the Earls of Ulster. Postcard published by the Union Castle Line.

THE UNION-CASTLE LINE INTERMEDIATE STEAMER "GLOUCESTER CASTLE." (7,999 TONS)

# GLOUCESTER CASTLE

*Gloucester Castle* was the third of the second 'G' class. She was built by the Fairfield Ship Building and Engineering Company of Glasgow and was launched on the 13th May 1911. Her maiden arrival at Capetown was on the 15th September 1911. With the advent of the First World War, she was requisitioned by the Admiralty in September 1914 and converted into a hospital ship. In this capacity *Gloucester Castle* served from the 24th September 1914 to the 9th September 1919. On the 31st March 1917 she was torpedoed by the German submarine UB32 whilst on service in the English Channel. She fortunately survived and was towed to Portsmouth for repairs. She was demobilised in 1920 and returned to the intermediate service. *Gloucester Castle* remained on this service for the next 22 years. On the 15th July 1942 she was attacked and sunk by the German raider *Michel* 750 miles from Ascension Island with the unfortunate loss of 93 lives.

**TECHNICAL DETAILS.** Identical to *Galway Castle* (page 33) except gross registered tonnage was 7,999.
*Gloucester Castle* was named after a castle in Gloucestershire.

UNION-CASTLE LINE INTERMEDIATE STEAMER "GUILDFORD CASTLE." 7,995 TONS.

# GUILDFORD CASTLE

*Guildford Castle* was the fourth of the second series of five 'G' class intermediate ships. She was built by Barclay Curlé and Company of Whiteinch and was launched on the 11th August 1911. Her maiden arrival at Capetown was on the 11th November 1911. She was requisitioned by the Admiralty in September 1914 and was converted into a hospital ship in line with three of her four sisters. She served in that capacity from the 22nd September 1914 to the 19th November 1918. *Guildford Castle* served in the Mediterranean and off the coast of East Africa, before she was released to her owners in 1920. She returned to the intermediate service for two years and then transferred to the Round Africa service. On the 30th May 1933 she collided with the Blue Funnel ship *Stentor* in the River Elbe, with the loss of three lives. She sank the following day.

**TECHNICAL DETAILS.** Identical to *Galway Castle* (page 33) except gross registered tonnage was 8,036.
*Guildford Castle* was named after a castle standing above Guildford in Surrey.

UNION-CASTLE LINE INTERMEDIATE STEAMER "LLANSTEPHAN CASTLE" (11,293 TONS)

# LLANSTEPHAN CASTLE

*Llanstephan Castle* was the sister of *Llandovery Castle* (page 37) and was built for the East Africa service. She was built by the Fairfield Ship Building and Engineering Company Limited of Glasgow and was launched on the 29th August 1913. Her maiden arrival at Durban was on the 2nd April 1914. In 1917 she was requisitioned as a troopship and was only used in this capacity for a year. She was used on the Cape mail route for two years before returning to the East Africa route in 1920. In 1939 she was converted from being coal-fired to oil-firing. In 1941 *Llanstephan Castle* was requisitioned by the Ministry of War Transport as a transport and supply ship. She remained in this role until 1944, when she was transferred to the Royal Indian Navy for use as an auxiliary ship. In September 1947 she returned to the East Africa service after a major refit. On the 1st March 1952 she arrived at the Newport yard of John Cashmore Limited for breaking-up. *Llanstephan Castle* served her owners for 38 years, the longest service in the Union-Castle Line history.

**TECHNICAL DETAILS.** Powered by quadruple expansion steam engines, developing 5,800 indicated horse power, driving twin screws, giving a maximum speed of 14 knots. Her length was 500 feet 5 inches with a gross registered tonnage of 11,293. She carried 460 passengers in three classes. *Llanstephan Castle* was named after a castle in Dyfed. Lord Kylsant, chairman of Royal Mail Steam Packet, was the lord of the manor.

UNION-CASTLE LINE EAST AFRICAN STEAMER
" LLANDOVERY CASTLE " (10,609 TONS).

# LLANDOVERY CASTLE

*Llandovery Castle* was the first Union-Castle Liner built for the Line's new owners, the Royal Mail Steam Packet Company, under the chairmanship of Sir Owen Cosby Phillips, later Lord Kylsant. She was built by Barclay Curlé and Company of Whiteinch and launched on the 3rd September 1913. She was built specifically for the London to East Africa route via the Suez Canal. Her maiden arrival at Durban was on the 6th March 1914. In December 1915 she was requisitioned by the Admiralty and converted into a hospital ship. On the 27th June 1918 she was torpedoed and sunk by the German submarine U86, 116 miles south west of the Fastnet Rock, with a loss of 234 lives. *Llandovery Castle* had a life of only four and a half years.

**TECHNICAL DETAILS.** Powered by quadruple expansion steam engines, developing 5,800 indicated horse power, driving twin screws, giving a maximum speed of 14 knots. Her length was 500 feet 1 inch with a gross registered tonnage of 11,423. She carried 450 passengers in three classes. *Llandovery Castle* was named after a castle on the Towey in Dyfed.

UNION-CASTLE LINE ROYAL MAIL STEAMER "ARUNDEL CASTLE" 19,023 TONS

# ARUNDEL CASTLE (3)

*Arundel Castle* (3) and her sister *Windsor Castle* (2) (page 39) were the last four-funnelled liners built. She was laid down in 1915 as the *Amroth Castle,* but work was suspended. *Arundel Castle* (3) was the Union-Castle Line's first steam turbine powered vessel. She was built by Harland and Wolff of Belfast and eventually launched on the 11th September 1919. Her maiden arrival at Capetown was on the 9th May 1921. In 1937 she was refitted and was re-engined and lengthened, losing two of her funnels in the process. On the 1st January 1940 she was requisitioned by the Ministry of Shipping for use as a troopship and it was not until September 1950 that she was returned to her owners, after a year-long post-war refit. *Arundel Castle* (3) served on the mail route until the 5th December 1958 when she made her final departure from Capetown to Southampton. On the 6th February 1959 she arrived at the Hong Kong yard of the Hong Kong Chiap Hua Manufactory Company for breaking-up. In her career of 37 years 8 months she had steamed a total of 3,475,565 miles.

**TECHNICAL DETAILS** (as built). Powered by single reduction geared steam turbines, developing 14,500 shaft horse power, driving twin screws, giving a maximum speed of 16 knots. Her length was 630 feet 5 inches with a gross registered tonnage of 19,023. As built she carried 870 passengers in three classes. *Arundel Castle* (3) was named after the castle in Sussex, the home of the Dukes of Norfolk. Postcard published by J. Arthur Dixon, of Newport, Isle of Wight.

THE UNION-CASTLE LINE ROYAL MAIL STEAMER "WINDSOR CASTLE" (18,967 TONS)

# WINDSOR CASTLE (2)

*Windsor Castle* (2), the sister ship of the *Arundel Castle* (3), was laid down in 1919, but not launched until 1921. She was built by John Brown and Company of Glasgow and she was launched on the 9th March 1921. Her maiden arrival at Capetown was on the 9th May 1922. In March 1937 she was sent to Harland and Wolff of Belfast for a refit, identical to that of her sister *Arundel Castle* (page 38). In September 1939 she was requisitioned by the Ministry of Shipping for use as a troopship. On the 23rd March 1943, whilst in a convoy 110 miles north west of Algiers, she was torpedoed and sunk by German aircraft, with the loss of one life.

**TECHNICAL DETAILS** (as re-built). Powered by single reduction geared steam turbines, developing 24,000 shaft horse power, driving twin screws, giving a maximum speed of 19 knots. Her length was 661 feet 3 inches with a gross registered tonnage of 19,141. She carried 580 passengers in three classes.

*Windsor Castle* was named after a castle in Berkshire, one of the homes of the Royal Family.

THE UNION-CASTLE LINE ROYAL MAIL MOTORSHIP "CARNARVON CASTLE" (20,063 TONS)

# CARNARVON CASTLE (2)

*Carnarvon Castle* (2) was a milestone ship for the Union-Castle Line. She was the first motorship and the first mailship over 20,000 gross registered tons. She was built by Harland and Wolff of Belfast and was launched on the 14th January 1926. Her first arrival at Capetown was on the 2nd August 1926. In October 1937 she was returned to her builders for rebuilding. She was lengthened by 56 feet and given more powerful ten-cylinder engines of 24,000 brake horse power. On the 8th September 1939 she was requisitioned by the Admiralty and converted into an armed merchant cruiser. H.M.S. *Carnarvon Castle* was in action against the German raider *Thor,* losing six of her crew before escaping. On the 29th November 1943, she became a troopship and served in this capacity until demobilised on the 1st January 1947. She returned to the mail service and remained on this service until her final departure from Capetown on the 18th June 1962. *Carnarvon Castle* (2) was sold for breaking up and on the 8th September 1962 she arrived at Mihara in Japan for that purpose.

**TECHNICAL DETAILS** (as built). Powered by Burmeister and Wain 4S DA eight-cylinder oil engines, developing 13,000 brake horse power, driving twin screws, giving a maximum speed of 16 knots. Her length was 630 feet 7 inches with a gross registered tonnage of 20,063. She carried 850 passengers in three classes. *Carnarvon Castle* was named after a castle at the south-west end of the Menai Straits in Gwynedd.

Postcard from a painting by John H. Fry, published by J. Salmon of Sevenoaks.

UNION-CASTLE LINE EAST AFRICAN STEAMER "LLANDAFF CASTLE" (10,786 TONS)

# LLANDAFF CASTLE

*Llandaff Castle* was built for the Round Africa intermediate service. She was built by Workman Clark and Company of Belfast and launched on the 10th August 1926. Her maiden arrival at Capetown was via the Suez Canal on the 26th February 1927. In 1939 she was converted from coal-firing to oil-firing. On the 26th December 1939 she was requisitioned by the Ministry of Shipping for use as a troopship. On the 30th November 1942 *Llandaff Castle* was torpedoed and sunk by the German submarine U177 off the coast of Zululand with the loss of two lives.

**TECHNICAL DETAILS.** Powered by quadruple expansion steam engines, developing 5,500 indicated horse power, driving twin screws, giving a maximum speed of 14 knots. Her length was 471 feet 2 inches with a gross registered tonnage of 10,763. She carried 321 passengers in two classes. *Llandaff Castle* was named after a castle in South Glamorgan.

UNION-CASTLE LINE INTERMEDIATE MOTORSHIP " DUNBAR CASTLE "

# DUNBAR CASTLE (2)

*Dunbar Castle* (2) was another of the Union-Castle Line's war losses and was built for the west coast intermediate route. She was built by Harland and Wolff of Glasgow and she was launched on the 31st October 1929. Her maiden arrival at Capetown was on the 1st July 1930. In December 1938 she was transferred to the Round Africa service. On the 9th January 1940 *Dunbar Castle* struck a mine north east of the Goodwin Sands and sank with the loss of nine lives.

**TECHNICAL DETAILS.** Powered by Burmeister and Wain 4S SA six-cylinder oil engines, developing 6,300 brake horse power, driving twin screws, giving a maximum speed of 14 knots. Her length was 471 feet 2 inches with a gross registered tonnage of 10,002. She carried 443 passengers in two classes. *Dunbar Castle* was named after a castle in East Lothian.

The UNION-CASTLE Royal Mail Motorship "WINCHESTER CASTLE" (20,000 tons)

# WINCHESTER CASTLE

*Winchester Castle* was an improved version of *Carnarvon Castle* (2). She was built by Harland and Wolff of Belfast and launched on the 19th November 1929. Her first arrival at Capetown was on the 10th November 1930. In April 1938 she was returned to her builders for rebuilding. Losing one of her funnels and given more powerful ten-cylinder engines of 24,000 brake horse power. On the 8th December 1940 she was requisitioned by the Ministry of Shipping and converted to a troopship. She was used in several theatres of war and it was not until 22nd April 1947 that she was demobilised, returning to the Cape route. With the arrival of *Windsor Castle* (3) (page 56) *Winchester Castle* was surplus to requirements. On the 9th September 1960 she left Capetown for the last time and was sold for breaking-up and on the 5th November 1960. She arrived at Mihara, Japan for that purpose.

**TECHNICAL DETAILS** (as built). Powered by Burmeister and Wain 4S DA eight-cylinder oil engines, developing 13,000 brake horse power, driving twin screws, giving a maximum speed of 16 knots. Her length was 631 feet 6 inches with a gross registered tonnage of 20,109. She carried 756 passengers in three classes.
*Winchester Castle* was named after Winchester castle in Hampshire.

The UNION-CASTLE Royal Mail Motorship "WARWICK CASTLE" (20445 tons)

# WARWICK CASTLE (3)

*Warwick Castle* (3) was a sister of the *Winchester Castle* (page 43). She was built by Harland and Wolff of Belfast and was launched on the 29th April 1930. Her maiden arrival at Capetown was on the 16th February 1931. In January 1938 she was returned to her builders for rebuilding. Losing one of her funnels and given more powerful ten-cylinder oil engines of 24,000 brake horse power. On the 8th January 1940 she was requisitioned by the Ministry of Shipping and converted to a troopship. On the 14th November 1942, after taking part in the invasion of North Africa, she was torpedoed and sunk by the German submarine U413 off the coast of Portugal, with the loss of 63 lives. *Warwick Castle* (3) was the largest Union-Castle vessel ever to have been lost by enemy action.

**TECHNICAL DETAILS** (as built). Powered by Burmeister and Wain 4S DA eight-cylinder oil engines, developing 13,000 brake horse power, driving twin screws, giving a maximum speed of 16 knots. Her length was 651 feet 5 inches with a gross registered tonnage of 20,445. She carried 746 passengers in three classes.
*Warwick Castle* was named after a castle eight miles from Stratford in Warwickshire.

"STIRLING CASTLE"

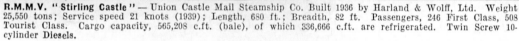

**R.M.M.V. " Stirling Castle "** — Union Castle Mail Steamship Co. Built 1936 by Harland & Wolff, Ltd. Weight 25,550 tons; Service speed 21 knots (1939); Length, 680 ft.; Breadth, 82 ft. Passengers, 246 First Class, 508 Tourist Class. Cargo capacity, 565,208 c.ft. (bale), of which 336,666 c.ft. are refrigerated. Twin Screw 10-cylinder Diesels.

# STIRLING CASTLE (2)

*Stirling Castle* (2) was the first mailship built to carry only two passenger classes. She was built by Harland and Wolff of Belfast and was launched on the 15th August 1935. Her maiden arrival at Capetown was on the 23rd February 1936. On a later passage in 1936 she broke the record for the fastest time to and from the Cape, which had been held by the Union Line's *Scot* (page 5) for 43 years. On the 19th October 1940 she was requisitioned by the Ministry of Shipping and converted into a troopship. She remained on trooping duties throughout the Second World War and was not demobilised until the 17th January 1947. *Stirling Castle* (2) was sent to her builders for a refit before returning to the Cape Mail route. She remained on this route until her final departure from Capetown on the 14th November 1965. She was sold for breaking-up and on the 3rd March 1966 arrived at Mihara, Japan for that purpose.

**TECHNICAL DETAILS.** Powered by Burmeister and Wain 2S DA ten-cylinder oil engines, developing 24,000 brake horse power, driving twin screws, giving a maximum speed of 19½ knots. Her length was 696 feet with a gross registered tonnage of 25,550. She carried 784 passengers in two classes.

*Stirling Castle* was named after a castle overlooking the River Forth in Scotland. Postcard published by Valentines and Sons of Dundee and London.

R.M.M.V. ATHLONE CASTLE

# ATHLONE CASTLE

*Athlone Castle* was the sister ship of the *Stirling Castle* (2) (page 45). She was built by Harland and Wolff of Belfast and launched on the 28th November 1935. Her first arrival at Capetown was on the 14th April 1937. On the 27th December 1940 she was requisitioned by the Ministry of Shipping for use as a troopship. She remained on trooping duties throughout the Second World War. She carried 148,113 persons on military service and was not demobilised until the 17th September 1946. *Athlone Castle* was sent to her builders for a refit and in May 1947 returned to the mail route. She remained on this route until her final departure from Capetown on 23rd July 1965. She was sold for breaking-up and on the 13th September 1965 she arrived at Kaohsiung, Taiwan.

**TECHNICAL DETAILS.** Identical to *Stirling Castle* (page 45) except her gross registered tonnage was 25,564.
*Athlone Castle* was named after a castle which stands on the River Shannon, Westmeath, Eire.
Postcard published by J. Salmon of Sevenoaks.

THE UNION-CASTLE LINE M.V. "DURBAN CASTLE" (17,388 tons)

# DURBAN CASTLE

*Durban Castle* was built for the west coast intermediate service. She was built by Harland and Wolff of Belfast and launched on the 14th June 1938. Her maiden arrival at Capetown was on the 18th January 1939. She was requisitioned by the Ministry of Shipping in December 1940 for use as a troopship. She served in the North African landings and other campaigns, before being demobilised in November 1946. In July 1947 she returned to the mail route and three years later she was placed on the Round Africa service. In March 1962 *Durban Castle* was sold to German breakers and on the 13th April 1962 she arrived at Hamburg for breaking-up.

**TECHNICAL DETAILS.** Powered by Burmeister and Wain 2S DA eight-cylinder oil engines, developing 16,000 brake horse power, driving twin screws, giving a maximum speed of 18 knots. Her length was 570 feet 7 inches with a gross registered tonnage of 17,388. She carried 555 passengers in two classes. *Durban Castle* was named after the town in South Africa.

Union-Castle
Line.

Union-Castle
Line.

# PRETORIA CASTLE (2)

*Pretoria Castle* (2) and her sister ship the *Edinburgh Castle* (3), (page 51) marked the return to steam propulsion. She was built by Harland and Wolff of Belfast and was launched on the 19th August 1947. Her maiden arrival at Capetown was on the 5th August 1948. In May 1965 she had a major refit, which gave her a new mast layout. On the 1st January 1966 *Pretoria Castle* (2) was sold to the South African Marine Corporation and renamed *S.A. Oranje*. She continued on the Cape mail run. In September 1975 she was sold to the Chin Tai Steel Enterprises Company of Kaohsiung Taiwan for breaking-up.

**TECHNICAL DETAILS.** Powered by double reduction geared steam turbines developing 35,000 shaft horse power, driving twin screws, giving a maximum speed of 22 knots. Her length was 717 feet 4 inches with a gross registered tonnage of 28,705. She carried 705 passengers in two classes. *Pretoria Castle* was named after the capital of South Africa. Postcard published by J. Arthur Dixon of Newport, Isle of Wight.

# S.A. Oranje

Here is the *Pretoria Castle* (2) in her new guise under South African Marine Corporation ownership.
The Postcard published by J. Arthur Dixon of Newport, Isle of Wight.

## UNION-CASTLE LINE
Royal Mail & Intermediate Services between
### ENGLAND & SOUTH & EAST AFRICA

Union-Castle Line advertising postcard from the 1950s.

R.M.S. EDINBURGH CASTLE, UNION CASTLE LINE
28,705 GROSS TONS    LENGTH 718FT.    SPEED 22 KNOTS    TWIN-SCREW

# EDINBURGH CASTLE (3)

*Edinburgh Castle* (3) and her sister *Pretoria Castle* (2) (page 48) were built to replace vessels lost in the Second World War. She was built by Harland and Wolff of Belfast and launched on the 16th October 1947. Her first arrival at Capetown was on the 23rd December 1948. In June 1965 she had a major refit which gave her a new mast layout. On the 7th May 1976 *Edinburgh Castle* made her final departure from Capetown. She was sold to the Chou's Iron and Steel Company and on the 4th June 1976 she arrived at Kaohsiung, Taiwan for breaking-up.

**TECHNICAL DETAILS.** Identical to *Pretoria Castle* (page 48).
*Edinburgh Castle* (3) was named after the castle overlooking the City of Edinburgh in Lothian.  Postcard published by J. Salmon of Sevenoaks.

Union-Castle
Line.

# KENYA CASTLE

*Kenya Castle* and her two sisters, *Rhodesia Castle* and *Braemar Castle*, (page 53) were the last intermediate ships built. She was built by Harland and Wolff of Belfast and launched on the 21st June 1951. Her first arrival at Capetown via Suez was on the 23rd May 1952. *Kenya Castle* was given an overhaul in 1961 which gave her a taller funnel with a domed top. She was withdrawn in April 1967 and laid up in the River Blackwater. In July 1967 she was sold to a company within the Chandris Shipping group of Piraeus Greece and renamed *Amerikanis* which means American Lady. *Amerikanis* had a year long refit at Piraeus and after the completion was placed on the service to New York and cruising. She cruised full time from 1970 until laid up at Eleusis, Greece in October 1996. In February 2001 negotiations were under way for *Amerikanis* to become a hotel ship in London's docks. This fell through and *Amerikanis* was sold to Indian shipbreakers.

**TECHNICAL DETAILS.** Powered by Parsons double reduction steam turbines, developing 14,400 shaft horse power, driving twin screws, giving a maximum speed of 18 knots. Her length was 556 feet 4 inches with a gross registered tonnage of 17,041. As built she carried 526 passengers in one class.
*Kenya Castle* was named after the East African country of Kenya.   Postcard published by the Union-Castle Line.

Union-Castle
Line.

# BRAEMAR CASTLE (3)

*Braemar Castle* (3) was the last intermediate ship built for the Union-Castle Line. She was built by Harland and Wolff of Belfast and launched on the 24th April 1952. Her maiden arrival at Capetown was on the 7th December 1952. She had a major overhaul in 1960 and was fitted with a taller domed funnel, like her two sisters. From June 1962 *Braemar Castle* (3) was placed on the London to Durban service via Suez. With the wind of change in Africa and jet air travel, *Braemar Castle* (3) and her sisters became redundant and they were withdrawn from service. *Braemar Castle* (3) was laid up in London Docks from November 1965. She was sold for breaking-up and on the 6th January 1966 arrived at Faslane for that purpose.

**TECHNICAL DETAILS.** Identical to *Kenya Castle* (page 52) except her gross registered tonnage was 17,029 and she carried 552 passengers in one class.
*Braemar Castle* (3) was named after a castle overlooking the River Dee in Grampian. Postcard published by J. Arthur Dixon of Newport, Isle of Wight.

# REINA DEL MAR

*Reina Del Mar* was built for the Pacific Steam Navigation Company of Liverpool. She was built by Harland and Wolff of Belfast and was launched on the 7th June 1955. She was built for the Liverpool to South America service. But this service came to an end in March 1964. On the 10th March 1964 she was sent to her builders and converted to a full-time cruise ship. On completion she was chartered to the Travel Savings Association founded by a Mr Max Wilson. She made her first cruise for her new owners in June 1964. Union-Castle Line managed *Reina Del Mar,* but they did not buy her until October 1973. This ownership did not last long, as she was sold to the Tung Cheng Steel Manufacturing Company and on the 30th July 1975 she arrived at Kaohsiung, Taiwan to be broken up.

**TECHNICAL DETAILS.** Powered by Parsons double reduction steam turbines developing 17,000 shaft horse power, driving twin screws, giving a maximum speed of 18 knots. Her length was 560 feet with a gross registered tonnage of 20,234. As built she carried 766 passengers in three classes. After rebuilding she carried 1,026 passengers in one class.
Postcard published by J. Arthur Dixon of Newport, Isle of Wight.

R.M.S. PENDENNIS CASTLE, *UNION CASTLE LINE*
28,500 GROSS TONS.    LENGTH 765 FT.    BEAM 83 FT. 6 INS.    LAUNCHED DECEMBER, 1957

# PENDENNIS CASTLE

*Pendennis Castle* was the last ship built for the Union-Castle Line by Harland and Wolff of Belfast, due to that company delaying her launching because of an industrial dispute. She was the first Union Castle mailship to be built with stabilisers. She was launched on the 24th December 1957. Her maiden arrival at Capetown was on the 15th January 1959. She had a uneventful life under the Union-Castle house flag, serving that line for 17½ years. On the 14th June 1976 she arrived at Southampton for the last time and was sold to the Ocean Queen Navigation Corporation of Panama and renamed *Ocean Queen*. She arrived at Hong Kong on the 9th August 1976 and laid up. At the end of 1977 she was sold again and renamed at first *Sinbad* and later *Sinbad 1*. Unfortunately she never carried a single passenger for her new owners and in April 1980 she arrived at Kaohsiung, Taiwan for breaking-up.

**TECHNICAL DETAILS.** Powered by double reduction steam turbines, developing 46,000 shaft horse power, driving twin screws, giving a maximum speed of 24 knots. Her length was 716 feet with a gross registered tonnage of 28,582. She carried 675 passengers in two classes.
*Pendennis Castle* was named after a castle in Falmouth in Cornwall.  Postcard published by J. Salmon of Sevenoaks.

# WINDSOR CASTLE (3)

*Windsor Castle* (3) was the largest mailship built for the Union-Castle Line. She was built by Cammell Laird and Company of Birkenhead and launched on the 23rd June 1959 by Queen Elizabeth the Queen Mother. *Windsor Castle's* maiden arrival at Capetown was on the 22nd August 1960. She made the final mailship departure from Capetown on the 6th September 1977, arriving at Southampton thirteen days later. In October 1977 *Windsor Castle* (3) was sold to a company within the John Latsis Group of Piraeus, Greece and renamed *Margarita L.* On the 3rd October 1977 she left for Piraeus for conversion into a luxury floating accommodation ship, for service at Jeddah, Saudi Arabia. In June 1991 *Margarita L.* returned to Greece and was laid up at Eleusis Bay where she still remains.

**TECHNICAL DETAILS.** Powered by Pametrada double reduction geared steam turbines, developing 45,000 shaft horse power, driving twin screws, giving a maximum speed of 23 knots. Her length is 730 feet with a gross registered tonnage of 37,640. She carried 823 passengers in two classes.
*Windsor Castle* (3) was named after a castle in Berkshire, one of the homes of the Royal Family.
Postcard published by J. Arthur Dixon of Newport, Isle of Wight.

UNION-CASTLE — The Big Ship Way between Britain and South Africa.

# TRANSVAAL CASTLE

*Transvaal Castle* had the dubious distinction of being the last passenger mailship built for the Union-Castle Line. She was built by John Brown and Company of Clydebank and was launched on the 17th January 1961. She was the first Union-Castle liner to carry tourist class passengers only and on the 1st February 1962 made her maiden arrival at Capetown. On the 1st January 1966 she was sold, along with the *Pretoria Castle*, (page 48) to the South African Marine Corporation Limited and renamed *S.A. Vaal*. She continued on the mail run until the 10th October 1977, when she made her last arrival at Southampton. She was sold to Festivale Maritime part of Carnival Cruise Lines of Miami and renamed *Festivale*. On the 29th October 1977 she left Southampton for Kawasaki Heavy Industries Limited yard in Japan, where she was converted into a cruise ship. In May 1996 she was renamed *Island Breeze* and chartered to Dolphin Cruise Lines. Dolphin Cruise Line was taken over by Premier Cruises in 1997 and *Island Breeze* was renamed *Big Red Boat III*. At the end of 2000 Premier Cruises got into financial difficulties and its ships were arrested.

**TECHNICAL DETAILS.** Powered by Pametrada double reduction geared steam turbines, developing 40,000 shaft horse power, driving twin screws, giving a maximum speed of 23 knots. Her length is 700 feet with a gross registered tonnage of 32,697. As built she carried 729 passengers in one class. *Transvaal Castle* was named after a province in South Africa. *Transvaal Castle* postcard published by the Union Castle Line.

# ROTHESAY CASTLE (2)

*Rothesay Castle* (2) was built as a fast refrigerated fruit ship for the Union-Castle Line. She was built by the Greenock Dockyard Company and she was launched on the 30th December 1959. She had an identical sister, the *Rotherwick Castle*. They were especially built to bring fruit from South Africa to the United Kingdom mainly apples, pears and grapes. During the South African winter they were frequently laid up in Southampton Docks. *Rothesay Castle* (2) was sold to Lloyd Uruguay and renamed *Laura* in 1975. In September 1980 she was sold for breaking-up at Gadani Beach, Pakistan.

**TECHNICAL DETAILS.** Powered by Burmeister and Wain 2S SA six-cylinder oil engine, developing 9,500 brake horse power, driving a single screw, giving a maximum speed of 16½ knots. Her length was 480 feet with a gross registered tonnage of 9,650. She had refrigerated space of 449,520 cubic feet.
*Rothesay Castle* (2) was named after a castle on the Isle of Bute. Postcard published by Roberts and Wrate Ltd of Portsmouth.

# GOOD HOPE CASTLE (2)

*Good Hope Castle* (2) was the last ship ever built for the Union-Castle Line. She was built by Swan Hunter and Wigham Richardson Limited of Wallsend and was launched on the 16th February 1966. She was built as a refrigerated fruit and mail ship. She had an identical sister, the *Southampton Castle*. In 1967 she had accommodation built on for 12 passengers, mainly for calls at St Helena and Ascension Island. On the 29th June 1973 she caught fire and was abandoned 35 miles south-east of Ascension. The fire was extinguished and she was towed to Antwerp and then to Bilbao for repairs. *Good Hope Castle* (2) did not return to service until May 1974. She was withdrawn in 1977 and with her sister, *Southampton Castle*, which had made the last arrival from the Cape on the 20th October 1977 were laid up in Southampton Docks. In February 1978 she was sold along with her sister, to Costa Lines of Genoa and renamed *Paolo C*, her sister was named *Franca C*. In 1984 *Paolo C*. was sold to Chinese ship breakers and on the 27th July arrived at Shanghai for breaking-up.

**TECHNICAL DETAILS.** Powered by Sulzer 2S SA eight-cylinder oil engines, developing 34,720 brake horse power, driving twin screws, giving a maximum speed of 25 knots. Her length was 545 feet with a gross registered tonnage of 10,538. She had refrigerated space of 380,313 cubic feet. *Good Hope Castle* (2) was another name for the castle at Capetown, South Africa. Postcard published by J. Arthur Dixon of Newport, Isle of Wight.

Union-Castle
Line.

H.M.H.S. GARTH CASTLE.

Union-Castle
Line.

# HMHS
# GARTH CASTLE

A rare postcard view of *Garth Castle* (see page 31) as a hospital ship. She was requisitioned by the Admiralty in November 1914 and based at Scapa Flow.

SOUTH AFRICAN ROYAL MAIL SERVICE.

A UNION-CASTLE LINER  THE UNION-CASTLE MAIL STEAMSHIP COMPANY, Limited.
DONALD CURRIE & Co., MANAGERS, LONDON.

A very rare early design postcard from the Union-Castle Line.

One of the very few Union-Castle postcards used to advertise the shipping line's services.

UNION CASTLE LINE S.S. "GAUL"

# GAUL

A very rare postcard published by Valentine's from the FGO Stuart collection. These were colour lithographed in Germany before the First World War. Here is the *Gaul* first of the 'G' class built for the Union Line in 1893. (See page 6.)

Union-Castle Line R. M. S. Saxon

# SAXON (4)

Another of the Valentine cards. This is the *Saxon* (4), built in 1899. (See page 22.)

# Index

**Braemar Castle** An American produced postcard of *Braemar Castle* (3) entering dock.
(See Page 53)

| | | |
|---|---|---|
| STIRLING CASTLE (2) | 15.08.1935 | 45 |
| ATHLONE CASTLE | 28.11.1935 | 46 |
| DURBAN CASTLE | 14.06.1938 | 47 |
| PRETORIA CASTLE (2) | 19.08.1947 | 48 |
| EDINBURGH CASTLE (3) | 16.10.1947 | 51 |
| KENYA CASTLE | 21.06.1951 | 52 |
| BRAEMAR CASTLE (3) | 24.04.1952 | 53 |
| REINA DEL MAR | 07.06.1955 | 54 |
| PENDENNIS CASTLE | 24.12.1957 | 55 |
| WINDSOR CASTLE (3) | 23.06.1959 | 56 |
| TRANSVAAL CASTLE | 17.01.1961 | 57 |
| ROTHESAY CASTLE | 30.12.1959 | 58 |
| GOOD HOPE CASTLE | 16.02.1966 | 59 |

# BIBLIOGRAPHY

Union-Castle and the War, 1914–1919, E. F. Knight, Union-Castle 1920
Union-Castle Chronicle, 1853–1953, Marischal Murray, Longmans 1953
Ships of the Union-Castle Line, Lawrence Dunn, Adlard Coles 1954
North Star to Southern Cross, J. M. Maber, T. Stephenson & Sons 1967
Great Passenger Ships of the World, A. Kludas, Patrick Stephens,
Six Volumes 1975–1992
The Cape Run, W. H. Mitchell & L. A. Sawyer, Terence Dalton 1984
Capetown Harbour, 1652 to the present, P. Newall, Portnet 1993
Union-Castle Line A Fleet History, P. Newall, Carmania 1999
Various issues of Ships Monthly, Sea Breezes, Southampton Docks
publications, Southern Evening Echo

# Arundel Castle (3)

A postcard from J. Arthur Dixon of *Arundel Castle* as re-built from her original four-funnelled design. (See Page 38.)